TOGETHER AND STRONG

TOGETHER AND STRONG

✦

Overcoming Fear in Relationships

Dr. Mary Franzen Clark

iUniverse, Inc.
New York Lincoln Shanghai

TOGETHER AND STRONG
Overcoming Fear in Relationships

Copyright © 2005 by Dr. Mary Franzen Clark

All rights reserved. No part of this book may be used or reproduced by any means, graphic, electronic, or mechanical, including photocopying, recording, taping or by any information storage retrieval system without the written permission of the publisher except in the case of brief quotations embodied in critical articles and reviews.

iUniverse books may be ordered through booksellers or by contacting:

iUniverse
2021 Pine Lake Road, Suite 100
Lincoln, NE 68512
www.iuniverse.com
1-800-Authors (1-800-288-4677)

All names and details have been changed to protect confidentiality. If names or situations resemble any living persons, it is purely coincidental.

ISBN-13: 978-0-595-37427-4 (pbk)
ISBN-13: 978-0-595-81819-8 (ebk)
ISBN-10: 0-595-37427-1 (pbk)
ISBN-10: 0-595-81819-6 (ebk)

Printed in the United States of America

To my husband, Dr. Thomas R. Clark, a person I have never feared.

Contents

INTRODUCTION 1

CHAPTER 1 FEAR 5
- *WHEN FEAR IS OUR FRIEND* 5
  - SHORT TERM FEAR REACTIONS 6
  - PROLONGED FEAR REACTIONS 7
- *FEAR AND VICTIMIZATION* 10
- *SOURCES OF FEAR—MISUSE OF POWER* 11
- *POWER AND FEAR* 13

CHAPTER 2 LIVING WITH FEAR 15
- *DOMINANT/SUBORDINATE SYSTEM AND HOW IT CREATES FEAR* . . 15
  - THE SACRIFICE STRATEGY 17
  - THE SUPPRESSION STRATEGY 19
  - THE STROKING STRATEGY 22
  - THE SUBMISSION STRATEGY 24
  - THE SEX STRATEGY 27
  - THE SCHOLARSHIP STRATEGY 29
- *SUMMARY* 33

CHAPTER 3 EMPOWERMENT 35
- *STARTING THE EMPOWERMENT PROCESS* 36
  - DETERMINE THE GAP 36
  - STRONG MODELS 38
- *FLEXING OUR MUSCLES* 39
- *BOUNDARIES* 41
- *SUPPORT SYSTEMS* 43

- *INNER STRENGTH AS EMPOWERMENT* 44
- *STEP ONE: VALIDATE REALITY AND FEELINGS.* 45
- *MAKING CHOICES.* 47

CONCLUSION 49

ACKNOWLEGMENTS

My deepest gratitude goes to the many men and women who have been my patients over the past years. They have taught me so much. It was the repetitive theme of fear that I heard in their stories that focused my attention on this topic.

I appreciate the wonderful group of men and women friends with whom I have shared my deepest thoughts and feelings. Their support and strength has helped me grow and provided incentive for writing this book.

Several friends took the time to review the manuscript and offered helpful suggestions and I am indebted to them. My editor, Letha Scanzoni, was a priceless person in the formation of this manuscript.

INTRODUCTION

Everyone wants happy, safe, healthy relationships. They are core to our happiness and contentment in life. They are core to our support systems. Our relationships give enrichment and meaning to life. No one enters a relationship thinking that it will go sour or become abusive. We believe, trust, and hope for a good outcome.

But sometimes it doesn't work out that way. All of the "data" about the other person—boss, friend, spouse, family member—may seem positive at first, or even for a number of years. However, there may be a "dark underbelly" that does not show up for a long time, or not until certain difficult circumstances—like financial stress, conflicts, loss, and anger—trigger it to come out. And that is when we usually wonder, "Where did this evil twin live all the time I knew you?" Many relationships start with loving, caring feelings between people—husband/wife, boss/employee, friend/friend, parent/child, etc. Then, for whatever reason, one person begins to hurt and oppress the other, making the relationship unsafe, and the element of fear sets in. For example, after five years of happy marriage, suddenly the husband becomes abusive; after working in a supportive environment for eight years, the boss begins making sexual advances; after being a favorite son, Mom suddenly begins verbally abusing her son.

As we observe a person's management skills breaking down and giving way to attack, anger, abuse, and unethical behavior, we become frightened and don't know what to do. We had no idea that our friend, family member, coworker, could behave this way.

At first, we are likely to see such fear-inducing intrusions as *exceptions* to the reality of our relationship experience. The person is just having a bad day, not the "usual." We rationalize the incidents that have made us afraid and write them off. Even when they occur more and more often, it is still difficult to conclude that this is how our friend, family member, spouse, really *is*. Yet, the name calling, the attacks, the physical and/or emotional abuse, threats, demeaning words, and unreasonable demands gradually seem to become normative. *Now* what do we do? This question is what this book seeks to answer.

If there is one place where fear does not belong, it is in close relationships. Yet, as fear finds its way into the relationships of spouses, friends, work colleagues, and parents and children, it poisons the relationship. Loving, caring relationships cannot exist and thrive when the people involved do not feel emotionally safe. The Bible says that love casts out fear (1 John 4:18). But I find also that fear has a way of casting out love. In this short book, divided into three sections, I'll show some ways to turn this around.

Section I defines the different kinds of fear—short-term and long-term. I spell out how some fears are helpful and necessary, but how some are destructive. Fear is not always bad—but it can be bad, especially in relationships. Now that fear has intruded what to do? These relationships may have years of emotional investment—but they have changed. It is not possible for loving, caring relationships to thrive when the people involved do not feel emotionally safe. What I have observed is that fear destroys that emotional safety. As a result, love stagnates, and the focus changes to do everything possible to eliminate the fear. If it can be made safe again, maybe the loving can return? One can practice "communication skills" all day, but if people are afraid, if fear exists, the skills are useless.

In Section Two I discussed the various strategies commonly employed to cope with the fearful behavior. Everyone hopes that the situation will change. The coping strategies were designed out of sincerity, the desire to have peace, to minimize the harm, to keep the relationships good. But, as we discover in Section Two, it doesn't turn out that way. The strategies often end up making us feel helpless, angry and depressed. The strategies often ultimately end up "feeding the monster" the other person has become and teaching them that if they continue to be abusive, demanding and threatening, they get their way—we back down, leave them alone, not make them accountable, they get their way, etc. It boomerangs. We never expected this. We were just trying so hard to make the relationship work; to move it back to the good thing it was before.

Accepting that the underbelly is here to stay is hard to acknowledge. The previous image of the other person—friendly, kind, happy, generous, fun, etc.—is still in our minds and hearts as "who they really are." Incorporating the negative sides is something that meets with resistance. But at some point in time, when we have been scared enough, or hurt enough, or angry enough, we must be truthful.

Then what? As we saw in Section Three, it means making decisions. Hard decisions. Sometimes it means divorce, or changing a job, or distancing from a family member, or setting strong boundaries for protection. It takes energy and strength to do these things. In Section Three we look at ways that people can obtain this strength and energy—from friends, professional assistance, community systems, spiritual supports, mentors, etc.—anything and anyone who can help empower us. We need to stand up and oppose the destructive and dangerous actions toward us. We cannot "work with" the abusive behavior any further—it is not going to change, and we cannot afford to let it kill us. We cannot let it push us into actions that we would regret—like revenge, attacking back, sabotaging, or self-destructing. We need to find sources of power to help free us from the abuse.

As was said in the beginning, fear can be a good and useful thing. It triggers the reaction to flee or fight. It tells us that something bad is happening and we need to protect ourselves any way possible. When we put our hand on a hot burner, the pain tells us to take it off—quickly! When our hearts are broken and our dignity is mangled by another person, it is time to remove ourselves—as quickly as possible! In a society and sometimes in a culture where women or weaker persons are not generally protected by those in power or by the laws, it takes a good share of "guts" to protect one's self. The fear needs to be channeled into empowerment. Section Three guides us to see some of the possible sources for empowerment—they are available, and they are important. Very few people make these changes alone.

It is this author's hope that as you read this book, that it has helped you to see any areas of your life where you may be caught in a fear/safety dilemma. Perhaps it made you think of someone you know who is caught and this book and/or you may be helpful to him/her. Think of a wife, a coworker, a friend, a family member, a neighbor, a member of your book club or Bible Study. It is egregious that anyone should live their lives in fear, feeling trapped in an unsafe situation. Too much help is available. Hopefully, if he/she can see the situation and can be truthful about it, that will be half way to solving it and reclaiming his/her life.

Please read each section in sequence. Do not rush to the end to find the solution without first obtaining a clear analysis of the problem. Discover the enemy first, and then learn to overcome it.

The presence of fear which poisons so many relationships is a common, historical, and continuing occurrence, and can happen to anyone in any intersection of life where two people cross paths. It is my hope and prayer that this book will help people to recognize the presence of fear, how destructive it is, and learn how to deal with it so healthy, healed, strong, happy relationships can happen.

1

FEAR

A mother sees a car speeding toward her child who has chased the family pet into the street. • A bank teller feels the cold metal of a gun pressed against her head, as the masked robber warns he'll shoot if she doesn't pack up the money faster. • A woman, checking her answering machine, is startled by a stranger's creepy voice: "I'm watching you!" • You're driving along the interstate one night when you see zigzagging headlights suddenly cross the median into your lane. • "I'm afraid I have bad news," the physician tells the young father. "The test results show the tumor is malignant." • A family awakens one morning to find threatening graffiti painted on their garage. • A police officer is knocking on your door. A glance at the clock tells you it's 5 a.m., and you realize your teenager has not yet come home. • The television program is interrupted by a news bulletin. A plane has crashed. You know that a friend was going to be flying that day.

WHEN FEAR IS OUR FRIEND

In all such situations, we immediately react with *fear*. Fear is a heightened level of alertness combined with physical readiness that stems from *a response to impending or actual danger*. We react that way whether the peril is physical, emotional, mental, economic, or social.

When fear strikes, the mind and body react immediately. All outside stimuli are blocked out except for the threatening source. The mind races. We think faster than usual. The body goes into action: adrenaline rushes, muscles tighten, the heart pounds, breath quickens, and blood flows to the extremities. All of these physical responses are telling us that we are in danger. Fear responses enable the flight-or-fight needs. This instant reaction to fear in a dangerous situation is normal and good. It is designed for our safety. It is a friend who protects us. If we don't respond with fear, we may open ourselves to being hurt by the threatening object.

In the above examples, in some cases fast thinking will protect us. In some cases fast action may protect us. While hiking in the Smoky Mountains, my friends and I came into the proximity of bear. Boy, did we get out of there fast! Our legs carried us with more speed than we thought we were capable of! Fear gave us the strength to run fast and protect ourselves.

So what does this have to do with relationships? What if the source of danger is a mate? A friend? A parent? A boss? A teacher? Someone we love or care for? This is not supposed to happen here!

Yet, simple observation will yield the unhappy truth that all too often people may love and fear someone at the same time. The relationship starts off as loving, caring, and respectful. But for some unknown and sometimes known reasons, one person begins to act in ways that generate fear—a rageful boss, a manipulative friend, an incestuous parent, an abusive mate. Fear—the emotion meant to protect us—rises toward someone we want to love, be with, and care about. What to do? This is the theme of this book.

SHORT TERM FEAR REACTIONS

The average person will experience many momentary fear responses every day. A lady drops a glass on the floor and jumps aside to avoid cutting her foot; a driver is cut off and swerves to avoid an accident; a child falls from a bike and the parent rushes out to help; a speaker is desperately trying to find misplaced notes an hour before the presentation.

These short-term reactions bring on the fear response of the mind and body listed above—heightened alertness, quick breathing, muscle tension, adrenaline, etc. When the situation is resolved, and the cause of the fear no longer exists, it will take a few minutes for the mind and body to return to a relaxed state (normal). All these are examples of the healthy function of fear in short-term situations. It is much like the power surge button on a hand mixer—meant to be used on a resistant lump of batter, but not to be run continuously or it will burn out the motor. The quick grip of fear protects us, alerts us and gets us through when life hands us a scary moment. If we are aware of fear and utilize it well, we will be healthy people.

Short-term fear usually is not a problem for relationships. In fact, sometimes it can be helpful to bring people closer together. For example, the husband jumps to protect his wife when she falls; a neighbor dials emergency when he sees smoke in another house; a girl screams for help when her friend injures herself; a mom grabs her child away from a falling object. When one person helps another in a crisis, it can strengthen their bond and make them realize how much they mean to one another.

The dynamics of short-term fear responses that make them *non-threatening* to relationships are:

- They are brief and allow the persons to return to a relaxed state quickly;

- The sources of threat are external to the relationship;

- Should a source of the short-term fear be from a loved person, it is unplanned, unintentional, and everyone is aware of this;

- It is not likely to happen again;

- There is no jeopardy to anyone's sense of safety, love or security with each other.

On the other hand, if the above conditions are not true, i.e., the harm is intentional, it happens over and over, the harming person does not acknowledge their responsibility nor attempts to stop it, then these short-term events can generate fear. If Mom has a bad day at work and is stressed, and drops a plate after dinner, it is upsetting for the children. However if the dropped plate makes Mom aware of her stress level and she takes steps to calm herself and it doesn't happen again, no harm. In this case, the children will be fine. But what if Mom throws dishes every time she has a "bad day" on some random basis? Each incident may be considered a "short-term fear" episode, but when they are repetitive, the children will learn to be afraid of Mom. They won't know if it might escalate to other types of angry acting out (will she hit them?) and they will be hyperalert to any signs that it will happen again. They will live in fear.

PROLONGED FEAR REACTIONS

Prolonged fear occurs in situations where the danger may be repetitive, or is on going, and is not resolved quickly (like Mom having a lot of "bad days"). For the person who is the object of their fearful behavior, the body maintains a faster heartbeat, muscle tension, rapid breathing, higher levels of adrenaline, hyper alertness. Prolonged fear may continue in varying degrees for days, weeks, or even years.

Marion lives in prolonged fear. Her husband is an alcoholic. She never knows when he will go on another binge that usually makes him violent. Normally he does not drink during the week, but it HAS happened. She knows the next explosion is just one drink away—and that could be Friday, tomorrow, or three weeks away. She is always tense, always in a state of fear. She can't really enjoy the "good" times because that would make her too vulnerable for when he is violent. She's always on eggshells.

When Marion's husband walks into the house, or when she talks to him on the phone, she never knows what to expect. She is watching for clues as to whether he has been drinking. Will there be peace at the dinner table? Will he yell at the kids? She never relaxes. The physical and emotional state of fear is (on some level or another) always constant for her.

As we can see from Marion, the symptoms of fear are continuously present—hyperalert, tense, easily startled, always thinking of how to protect herself. One of the major problems with prolonged fear is that the body does not fully return to a normal state, to relax, to heave a sigh of relief, to exist in a state of safety and security. We all know people who can be described as being wound "tighter than a Swiss watch." Why? They are probably people who are living with fear on a daily basis. The tense muscles can usually be seen in the face, the clenched hands, the jumpy feet, etc. These people would love to relax, but until the source(s) of threat is diminished or gone, the prolonged state of fear will remain.

Angie is another example of what it is like to live in prolonged fear. She was the object of incest from the age of six until eleven. Then her father left home—no more threat of abuse. One would think Angie finally found relief from fear and could relax. But not really. Her father still lives in her town. Even at age 25, whenever she turns a corner, there is the possibility of running into him. Will she meet him in the grocery store today? Or at the post office? The tension never completely subsides. She tries to plan her errands when she knows he is at work. Should she see someone who even resembles her father, she has flashbacks and the fear is the same as in childhood days.

Donna is a single mother. She has no one upon whom she can rely for help, either financial or with babysitting. She found a good-paying job six years ago which was sufficient to buy a small house, a used car, and have medical benefits. Recently, Donna discovered her boss is having marital problems. Lately he has been moody. Finally, he confided to Donna over lunch one day that he no longer loved his wife. He wanted Donna to fulfill his sexual needs. Donna was stunned. Would she refuse and put her job in jeopardy? Donna is in a dilemma. She now lives in fear. She experiences anxiety on the way to work each morning. Recent upper GI tests showed the beginning of an ulcer.

The characteristics of prolonged fear that is generated from within a relationship are:

- No end in sight;
- No relief, no relaxation;
- Confusion;
- Elevated physical and emotional tension;
- A loss of trust in people and/or the world;
- Loss of safety;
- Constant vigilance;
- "Walking on eggshells," unpredictability.

In the situations of Marion, Angie and Donna, in each case a bond developed—love, affection, trust, caring, and/or sharing. Then something changed. A husband became violent; a father used his power to hurt his daughter sexually and emotionally; a secure and predictable employee/boss relationship turned unsafe. One partner began to poison the relationship. We cannot always assume why the partner does this, nor can it be predicted when this may happen. All we know is that what was once safe is now fearful. As we peel away the layers of each story, it becomes clear that each person wants to continue to feel safe with the important person in his/her life. However, fear will reduce, destroy, or severely alter the ability to care or love.

Let's look at the stories again. Marion's husband did not become overtly alcoholic until the fourth year of their marriage. In the beginning there was love. A child was born. They had some good years together. Then, he lost his job. Financial pressures closed in. That was when the drinking and violence began. Marion's husband began taking his anger and helplessness out on Marion. Fear entered into a once-loving relationship.

Angie loved her Mom and Dad. They were a happy family—until Mom left for another man. Dad became angry and bitter. Because Angie looked so much like her mother, Dad took out his anger and sexual frustration on her. She had to continue to live with him, but it was so confusing and difficult when she loved him and depended on him, but feared him at the same time.

Donna's boss was a fair man. He allowed her to take time off when her daughter was ill. He seemed to understand the situation. He was kind. What a surprise when she discovered there were strings attached to her ideal boss. Her normal quick step slowed down in the mornings on the way to work. Her enthusiasm was deflated by fear. Her respect for her boss was poisoned by fear.

I could relate more stories like these but the basic picture is the same. In each case, the person initially experienced respect, love and happiness with a primary person. But, gradually, insidiously, subtly (in some cases), the relationship was infiltrated with fear. These people ended up loving and fearing the same person. What a mixture of emotions! What are they to do? Fear has taken over like a creeping paralysis. The relationship has changed. Is there a solution?

Day after day, I hear people in these dilemmas make statements such as:

- "I'm afraid of him. I can't say 'no' to my husband."

- "I can't cross my boss."

- "Do I dare speak up for myself?"

- "I'm afraid I will create a conflict and be hurt even more."

- "I don't want to disagree. She may retaliate."

- "I don't dare express how I really feel—it's too scary."

When fear exists months, years, with no end in sight, it has lost its helpful effects (flight/fight strength), and starts to be destructive. Fear can limit, stop, stifle, distort, sabotage, and detour men and women from living life freely, safely and fully. When a woman fears her husband she cannot love him as totally as she would like. A fearful child who has learned from her father to not trust him has difficulty going to him for the help most children need from parents. A fearful employee cannot produce as efficiently as she could otherwise. When fear persists, an individual cannot be the expressive, happy, content, creative, growing person he/she would like to be. And they certainly cannot be safe.

FEAR AND VICTIMIZATION

The person who is generating the fear in us often becomes the focus of our attention. We can easily feel victimized by their power to induce fear. Angie feared her big, powerful father. Donna feared her boss because he had the power to cut off her income. Marion's husband wielded power in her home because of the chaos he created and she had little control over it. All of these people feel like victims; all of them live in fear.

The longer the victimization continues, the more power is attributed to the victimizer. The bigger the hurtful person becomes (in the victim's eyes), the more helpless and victimized the individual feels. The vicious cycle is clear. Over time, the effects are devastating. We have heard of women who have killed their husbands after years of pent-up rage caused by battering. Newspaper articles tell of fired employees returning for revenge on oppressive employers. Some people internalize the victimization and commit suicide.

Before a person ever reaches this "last straw" point, depression often is a common symptom. Depression occurs when one experiences prolonged helplessness (fear), and internalizes it because the person is afraid to deal with the source. Anxiety (or panic attacks) is sometimes a delayed response to past fears that have been suppressed (buried within). Eating disorders are a common reaction to fear of being controlled and the control of food compensates for the fear.

A friend of mine who has lived in fear more years than she cares to remember pointed out that she would not have recognized herself in this book if she had read it five years ago. She would have stopped reading it, or thought it referred to someone else. She stressed to me that even when her life was most scary, her fear was so suppressed that she would have denied it, even when symptoms were hitting her squarely between the eyes. It is difficult to admit feeling fear, living with fear. It is so important for friends, counselors, and therapists to be able to recognize and name it when fear is present.

SOURCES OF FEAR—MISUSE OF POWER

Power, in and of itself, is a neutral entity. Much like nuclear power—it can be used to light a city or it can be used to make bombs. It is what we DO with it what makes power creative or destructive. *Fear, then, occurs initially when the one who is in a position of power uses it to oppress, dominate or take advantage of another.*

A sound, healthy relationship cannot be built upon an unequal, lop-sided, dominant/subordinate power structure—whether it is in the home, on the job, in a personal relationship, in the church, or in society. In adult/adult relationships, it is important that there be an equal sharing and positive use of power in order for the relationships to be safe (free of fear). One person may have more social power, for example, but the other knows it will never be used to oppress. One may have more financial power, but the other knows it will never be used for leverage, humiliation, or for getting one's own way. Safety cannot exist when power is misused.

Even little children (who have no power) need to know that Mom's and Dad's power is used for their protection, safety and well being. Mom and Dad will not use their power to oppress them, hurt them, or leave them vulnerable in a world where they cannot meet their own needs. Good parents will use their power in such a way as to gradually share it with the growing child, so that when the child reaches adulthood, he/she is clearly aware of how power is to be used—for protection, to generate safety, for the good of one's self and the other person.

When power is misused, the "good" is aborted. Jim and Karen, a middle-class, church-going couple came in for counseling. When they described their lifestyle, a definite pattern became apparent. Jim was the dominator, she the subordinate. Jim exerted his power, made all decisions. Karen was expected to submit to his wishes. She had no say about anything. Money was spent to meet Jim's needs. Left over money was for the children. Vacations were at the place of Jim's choosing, whether or not it was suitable for the children. Their daily routine pivoted around his timetable. His moods were to be accommodated without question.

His reason for coming to counseling with Karen was that their sexual relationship was not what he wanted it to be. He complained that Karen expressed no interest in sex. Karen's story was that, because she was left out of decisions, because Jim did not care about her needs, feelings, ideas, she felt like a victim. Karen feared Jim and that made it difficult to be sexually vulnerable to him. In Jim's opinion, did Karen even think she had a right to intrude into his position as head of the household? Besides, what did her issues or the children's needs have to do with sex? He had no mind to share power with her and that was the end of the story. Needless to say, it was next to impossible to pursuade Jim that his intimidating abuse of power was destroying the safety of their relationship.

Jim created an atmosphere of fear in their home. He acted as a dictator. No one was allowed to defy him. The result was a wife who lived in fear because she didn't feel safe. Consequently, she had no desire to be sexual with him. How could she muster up any amount of desire to expose her most intimate self to someone who only used her for his own gratification? It never dawned on Jim that his oppressive attitude toward Karen caused her to feel less loving, caused her to be afraid of him. Karen's choice to withdraw sexually was the one area where she could exert her own power—to protect herself. Her fear was casting out her love.

Here are some broader examples of dominant/subordinate situations that can generate fear.

- Smaller people afraid of bigger people (physical size power);
- One nation afraid of another which has more weapons (destructive power);
- A minority group fears the majority group (political, legal power);
- A non-favored child moves aside for a favored child (power by delegation of an authority figure);
- The less athletic teen yields to the one with more acclaim (status power);
- The poor are victimized by the rich (money as power);
- The less attractive employee is passed for promotion (appearance power);
- The high school graduate is intimidated by the Ph.D. (knowledge as power).

And the list could go on. Wherever there is a disparity in the power level of one over another, there is the potential for the powerful one to use it to make the less powerful person a victim—to feel "big" like the "king of the mountain." If we hear enough daily news reports of victimization, we receive a clear message that the dominant/subordinate system is alive and well in countries, in homes, in churches, in institutions, businesses and relationships.

POWER AND FEAR

Fear in relationships exists because of the misuse of power. Only a person who has some type of power or authority can threaten another person. The list (above) of sources of power can generate an endless possibility of examples of misuse of power and resulting victims. It is unfortunate that in most societies, the majority of power brokers are male and the majority of victims are women, children and minorities. Most women and minorities in victim situations (physical, social, legal, financial, etc.) do not feel able to protect themselves and/or truly can't protect themselves. Most mechanisms for justice have been designed by males and are geared to the needs of the people in power.

Religion does not exempt people from the ravages of the misuse of power. In fact, it often supports the injustices from the secular power systems. For example, in fundamentalist Christian families, men might abuse their wives, humiliate them, disrespect them, demean them and justify it under the theory of "headship" of the man (as we saw with Jim). Because "headship" is interpreted in the Western, political, capitalistic system rather than in the Christlike system it sets up the man to have power which is and can be misused for whatever ego needs exist—and justify it. For this reason, it often takes Christian couples longer to admit a problem and to seek help. By the time they do go for help the damage is fairly imbedded, and the prolonged fear has become a lifestyle.

Living in fear has consequences. A victim cannot feel safe, cannot love, and cannot be intimate. Sometimes I ask people, "What is the most important thing to a child?" Usually they say, "To be loved." I agree that love is important, but if a child does not feel safe, he/she cannot be emotionally open to be loved. Safety is the cornerstone on which love can be built. When parents (or anyone else) abuse their power, a child cannot feel safe. When I ask couples, "What is the most important element in your relationship?" they usually answer, "Love" as well. Why, then, do people who claim to love each other are having so many conflicts? Because they probably do not feel safe with each other, and if they do not feel safe, the love is useless.

When couples present for counseling (usually at the urging of the victim), the power imbalance must be addressed to work on the basic element of safety. If the power partner realizes that he/she is abusing their position, sees the damage it creates in the victim and chooses to relinquish it in order to have the relationship, then a healthy relationship is possible. If the power partner only wants to have his/her power justified, and is not willing to give it up, nothing more can be done. Sadly, this happens all too often. Sometimes I ask the Power Male, "Do you really want your wife to be afraid of you?" The confusion in their eyes says it all.

Fear is alive and well in all phases of our society and throughout the world. Being an object of misused power is probably the underlying reason many people seek psychological help—whether they are aware of it or not. If this is not identified, any other objectives of treatment will not succeed. The goal is to achieve relationships where each person can be safely in control of his/her own life. Only then can we *choose* to share our lives with others, to form relationships free of fear. The need for primary bonding is universal for people, but it can only happen in safe settings, free of fear.

2

LIVING WITH FEAR

Fear and love are opposites. When we experience fear, we are in the presence of danger or threat. When we love, we are in the presence of safety, affirmation, and trust. These two emotions are not meant to abide together. One usually gives way to the other. Since being safe is more important than being loved, the fear will take primary focus.

In this section, we will consider the various ways people deal with the dilemma of feeling both love and fear toward the same person. Some phrases people use to express this dilemma are:

"I don't want to leave. I care about him/her."
"I have a lot invested in our relationship—I don't want to leave."
"I don't think I could find anything better. I'd like to stay."
"I can't change him/her, but I love him/her."

In your mind, picture a scale. On one side is safety (which permits love). On the other side is fear (which destroys love). In the center is the person caught between loving and fearing the same person at the same time. Which side will win? The person caught in this dilemma often wants desperately to make sure the safety side wins. The objective is, "If I can figure out how to reduce the fear side, and increase the safety side, then love can happen again."

DOMINANT/SUBORDINATE SYSTEM AND HOW IT CREATES FEAR

In Section One we saw a list of factors that can make some people more powerful than others—money, status, physical power, knowledge, weapons, favoritism, appearance, etc. In our present social system, based on a dominant/subordinate structure, subordinates will be the losers. Our social, legal, and economic system does not support or promote equal, cooperative relationships. Rather, it promotes competition, winning, and abuse of power. There are so many examples of people abusing others economically in order to "succeed"—underpaying workers, running off with pension money, not providing for worker safety, buying and selling slaves, threatening people with job loss to extract more labor, making illegal loans so stockholders lose out, etc.

Many couples who present for marital counseling are often engaged in dominant/subordinate issues, such as with Jim and Karen (Section One). Jim wanted everything his way, did not want to be bothered with the needs of Karen and the children, and would make their lives miserable if anyone foiled his wants and needs. Many people do not know any other way to relate.

Generally, it is the one who is hurting, who does not feel safe, who seeks help, to make the counseling appointment. I often say that there are three reasons people are ready to make changes—when they are hurt enough, are scared enough, or are angry enough. When Karen was scared and hurt and angry enough (in this case all three), she made the call to get help. She could no longer deny the degree of abuse of power and the fear it was generating. I have never had the experience of someone walking in my office and saying, "I have too much power and I am using it abusively and I must stop doing this." No. It is the victim of the abuse of power who wants the change. Most of the time, people, like Karen, hope to keep the relationship, but do not know how to deal with the fear to make it safer.

People involved in the dominant/subordinate system who feel victimized and fearful generally devise some creative and well-intentioned methods to help increase the safety end of the scale. Essentially, they try to *adapt* to the fear/safety dilemma. These adaptations—

1. are employed for the purpose of securing personal safety;

2. are employed to reduce the effects of fear;

3. are employed to make the relationship successful.

They want the relationship to succeed, to reduce conflict, to make peace, to create cooperation, to have the relationship be the happy, enjoyable relationship it was before. These strategies come out of the caring, loving heart of partners who just want the relationship to be better. They could never know ahead of time that in fact they end up "feeding the monster."

THE SACRIFICE STRATEGY

The Sacrifice Strategy is used when the subordinate person sets aside his/her own needs to give full attention to the needs of the dominator. The goal is to *please the powerful person,* to make sure his/her needs are satisfied, to the point where he/she will have no reason to be angry or threatening.

The system works this way:

- Suppress or deny one's own needs;

- Discover the needs of the dominator through careful observation;

- Satisfy all the dominator's needs any way possible;

Goal: When all the dominator's needs are met, all will be safe.

Sounds like this should work, doesn't it? At first, the partner/child/employee sacrifices out of caring to make the partner happy. But over time, the sacrificer finds out that the sacrifices are not appreciated, and, in fact, the dominator expects more sacrificing. The dominator gets angry and threatening when the subordinate does not continue to sacrifice. The sacrificing is clearly a one-way street, builds resentments and creates victim feelings.

During the first year on the job, Charles was happy to accept extra responsibility, work a little longer, and go the extra mile. Then one day it dawned on Charles that the company was getting executive-level work for middle management pay. Resentment set in. The feeling of victimization grew. If Charles ever resisted the requests for extra work, the boss would accuse him of being unmotivated, a slackard, and not interested in promotion. Charles began to fear his boss.

In the example of Karen and Jim, at first Karen adored Jim. She put him on a pedestal and strived to please him. She never asked Jim for anything and, of course, Jim never bothered to give anything. When he started leaving her and the children out of all the decisions, Karen developed more and more fear, and sacrificed more and more to try to abate it. She and the children were entirely dependent on Jim. After years of depleted giving, what Karen once gave freely now is dispensed because she is afraid.

Karen has looked after, done for, given up, and put up with the needs of her husband at the expense of meeting her own. She may have bought into the acronym "JOY—Jesus first, Others second, Yourself last." And has she ever been last! She is so "last" that she has lost herself. She eventually hated him because of his demands and hated herself for violating her own needs. The fear and anger were destroying her and destroying the relationship.

Most of us are familiar with the teaching, "Love your neighbor *as* yourself" (Matthew 19:19, italic added). Subordinates who take the road of the Sacrifice Strategy to seek safety are not obeying this principle. The Sacrifice Strategy requires, "Love your neighbor *more* than yourself." Instead of "Do unto others as you would have them do unto you," it ends up, "Do for others so they don't do unto you."

It is difficult to know exactly when well-intentioned sacrifice turns into resentment and when resentment turns into victimization. Karen believed, particularly from her Baptist church and her Russian mother, that sacrifice kept women safe and it was the right thing for them to do. Sacrifice is the way to avoid hurt and punishment. However, what no one told her was that the internalized anger, the loss of self, the prolonged fear would brew inside of her and cook up a deadly poison. It destroyed Karen almost beyond the point of repair.

As a disclaimer, in most healthy relationships, all parties make sacrifices, compromises and step outside themselves to care for and help each other. Men and women, friends, parents and children, bosses and employees all give and take with each other. There is no score keeping in the presence of love and safety. There is no threat of punishment or fear in a secure environment. There is no power play between the people involved. They are equally respectful and caring. There are no winners and losers. (Even in para-military corporate or institutional or religious settings, this can be achieved between people of different "levels" of function.)

If the motive for sacrifice is to insure safety, fear is in the driver's seat. The price for sacrificing to obtain safety is too high. The subordinate pays dearly, silently, and will eventually erupt like a volcano, or will implode, often with suicide or severe illness. By the time Karen came in for therapy, the damage was so extensive it was difficult for her to have hope or motivation for change.

' Friends or family who talk to Karen may have heard the clues from her that suggest she is caught in the Sacrifice Strategy:

"I feel left out."
"My husband and children take up most of my time."
"I have no time for myself."
"I don't know what else I ca do."
"I can't—it would really upset my husband."

All of these are hints that Karen is unable to express her degree of fear. She had to rationalize or minimize the abuse of power in order to get up every morning and function. But the truth is, she lived in daily fear of Jim—his emotional abuse, treating Karen like she did not exist, or when he did acknowledge her, was demeaning and shaming toward her.

If the Sacrifice Strategy is the only way Karen knows to deal with the daily fear she feels, can she give it up? Not unless she is able to risk Jim's retaliation if she stops it; not unless she may risk the marriage to stop it. The counselor has the difficult challenge of shifting the power in the relationship to be more equal, so that each person can be safe. Will Jim see the destructive effect of his ego-centered power? Will Karen value herself enough to stop a destructive coping skill? Can they relate to each other with enough respect, integrity, and shared power to allow the love they once shared to operate again? Can they, will they, change this deadly dance?

THE SUPPRESSION STRATEGY

In the Sacrifice Strategy, the subordinate person gives up everything about themselves—feelings, thoughts, needs, identity, self—in response to the fear they feel toward the dominant person in his/her life. The Suppression Strategy is not quite as total or overwhelming as the Sacrifice Strategy. Here the basic goal is to *avoid conflict*, disagreement or disapproval of the dominant person who has the power to make one's life unsafe. It is safer to push down one's own feelings/ideas than to be pushed down by the disapproval of the dominator. The greater the power gap between the dominator and the subordinate, the greater and more frequent the suppression.

The steps of the Suppression Strategy work like this:

1. Continuously check out what the dominator thinks/feels to know what NOT to disagree with.

2. Suppress any opinions and feelings that MAY create disagreement.

3. Let the dominator feel that his/her opinions and feelings are the only ones that matter, the only ones that are correct.

Goal: When there is no disagreement, the dominator is happy and the subordinate feels safe.

How many of us have hesitated to talk to a superior about something which we knew the superior did not want to hear? Rather than put ourselves in jeopardy, silence was the wisest choice. Suppression for safety is the only choice in the face of fear on some occasions, whether one is facing a Nazi guard, a temperamental boss, a moody wife, an opinionated professor, an angry parent. But this kind of suppression out of fear should not be the daily routine in our relationships. It reminds us of the Emperor's New Clothes—never tell the king what he does not want to hear!

There is so much intensity when I meet with women, employees, students, and other subordinate people, and hear their stories about the dominant persons they are afraid of. The enthusiasm with which they wave their arms while telling the stories! The volume in their voices! The strength in their words! Except that what they are sharing is what they would *like* to have said or done. What they really did was quite the opposite—suppressed. When the dominator is not present, the real ideas/feelings come out. Subordinate people who use the Suppression Strategy usually *are* aware of what they feel and think—but if voicing these things could jeopardize the fear/safety scale, nothing is said. (Note: People who use the Sacrifice Strategy mentioned above don't have enough "life" or awareness of themselves left in them to do this type of ranting and raving when the dominators are absent. The loss of "self" is so extensive that their feelings are on the other side of the Grand Canyon.)

In a situation of prolonged fear, if a person feels constrained against expressing their thoughts/feelings, they may eventually think, "Why should I *have* any opinions when they only get me into trouble?" A subordinate can devalue their feelings and thoughts when they are suppressed long enough. For example, children who grow up in alcoholic homes learn early that what they feel and think is not only unimportant to the parents (who are enmeshed in their own addiction and co-dependency issues), but that their feelings may even threaten what little approval and safety they may have. An alcoholic home is not a safe home emotionally. If the child expresses his/her feelings, it just may make things worse. So, the child learns to block out the feelings. Keep them inside. It is easier and safer that way.

Thus, children who may have grown up in homes that were alcoholic or abusive or neglectful or dysfunctional, where disagreement with the parent(s) constituted jeopardy of their safety may grow up to be adults who have a great deal of difficulty identifying their own feeling and opinions. These people are perfect "pigeons" for a relationship with a controlling, power-oriented dominator. Even if they meet someone who is egalitarian, they still fear that opening up their thoughts/feelings will not be safe.

I recall my conversation with Michael. He went on and on in an animated description of what his alcoholic mother did to him. Though Michael lived alone, his mother called often and made demands on him. Anything Michael said, she attacked and criticized. She imposed upon and invaded Michael's feelings and integrity. After I heard enough to get the picture, I asked Michael how he felt about her cruel remarks? What made him so compliant to her demands?

"I had no choice!" Michael answered.

"How do you feel about not making your own choice?" I asked.

"She does this to me all the time," Michael emphasized.

I persisted. "How do you feel when your mother does this to you?"

"She is selfish. That's why she does it."

"Michael, stop focusing on your mother and look inside yourself. What do YOU feel when your mother does this? Describe at least one feeling YOU have about your mother's behavior."

"Something I feel? (Pause) I'm a little upset, maybe."

"A little? It sounds like it is hard to admit how you really feel."

Can you hear how distant Michael's feelings are? How fearfully he exposes them? People caught in the Suppression Strategy will, over a period of time, push down their own feelings so often that, eventually, they become filled with resentment, anger and helplessness. Even though these feelings are there, they are more likely to say:

"My husband thinks I should…"

"My boss likes it when it…"

"It's easier when I don't…"

"It really doesn't matter what I think of…"

"Whatever you want…"

These subordinates have been trained well and have learned that what they think/feel does not matter, or worse, may generate a hurtful power play by the dominant. They are unaware of what all the suppressed feelings are doing to them. It is like having a cavity in a tooth and, while one continuously pumps Novocain into it to kill the pain, the cavity only gets worse.

If Michael (and others like him) gets closer to his anger, his fear of expressing it will come out in remarks like:

"It isn't polite to say how I feel…"

"Why should I bother to tell anyone how I feel?"

"It won't change anything if I say how I feel."

They are so focused on the expected anger/disapproval of the dominant, that any ownership of their feelings is scary. We can see the helplessness in the above statements. Hopefully, at some point in treatment, people will learn that saying how they feel is not to change the dominant, but to reduce their helplessness as a subordinate. They eventually learn that conflict and disapproval can be traversed; they can de-power the dominant by empowering themselves (to be discussed more in Section Three). If they can reduce the fear of the dominant's expected responses, they can increase their validation of themselves.

Helping Michael reconnect with his feelings/thoughts will be a slow, careful process to not feel overwhelmed. The "flood" of feelings he has kept in needs to be released gradually. In situations where people have lived in prolonged fear, we therapists need to respect the fact that the Suppression Strategy has kept them safe for a long time, especially if some of that time was childhood. Michael will learn eventually that being *in* touch with his feelings/thoughts will make him safer as an adult, but this will be a new "language" and a whole new way of life for Michael.

THE STROKING STRATEGY

The Stroking Strategy is essentially: *earn brownie points*! Then, when something goes wrong (in the dominator's opinion, of course), the scale will not tip too far on the fear side. The victim builds up enough "points" on the safety side to cushion any damage done by the dominator. After all, how can a dominator retaliate too much against someone who has been so wonderful?

The system proceeds this way:

1. "Mind read" to determine all the things that will please the dominator.

2. Do everything possible to please the dominator.

Goal: When the dominator is pleased and happy, others will feel safer.
The secretary may get the coffee, shop for the boss' wife, lie about his long lunch hours, etc. just to insulate herself against the day when she makes an error on a letter, misunderstands a message, or says a wrong word. When this happened in the past, the boss would explode and attack her with shaming words. Her thinking is that if she has stroked him enough, she may prevent the attack from happening again.

Debbie grew up in a home where Dad was Napoleon II. She loved him, needed him, and set out to please him (as most children do). She tried very hard. She waxed his care (she forgot the chrome); she excelled in sports (he never attended a game); she earned a 3.8 grade average (why not a 4.0?); she tried to look pretty for him (her sister was prettier), etc. The message was clear. No matter what she did, it wasn't good enough. He hurt her over and over again. His lack of approval crushed her. She grew to fear his inspections and criticisms.

Then Debbie met and married John, her college sweetheart. John was one great fellow. He loved and adored Debbie. But Debbie's fear of her father's disapproval carried over into her marriage, causing her to also fear John. If she failed to please John (or, determined for herself that she failed to please him), she feared John would become Napoleon III. John did nothing to merit this fear. It was a displacement from the intensely painful relationship with her father. When Debbie had her first baby, she quit work. This required her to be dependent on John. Now the parallel was even closer to her relationship with her father, and more fear was generated.

Finally, Debbie and John came for marital counseling. John was confused. Nothing he did seemed to satisfy her. He was at a loss as to how to win Debbie's love and trust. Debbie felt worthless, didn't trust John, was hyperalert and always suspicious. She outdid herself with fancy dinners, caring for the children, and keeping an immaculate home. John's shirts were always pressed and ready. But no matter how much John praised Debbie, Debbie never believed/trusted it.

Debbie was doing all her hard work for the wrong reason. She was trying to make her self feel safe with John—based on her father's criteria. There was no data that John would hurt her. Still, she spent her days in fear. In her mind, if she danced right and performed well, played the Stroking Strategy, there would be no threat to her safety. She was building up points against the day when John would emotionally slice her up like her father. That day never came. John never did. But simply being a man and having more financial and physical power than she generated fear in Debbie.

Whether fear is only perceived (as in Debbie's case with John), or real, (as in Debbie's case with her father), subordinates caught in the Stroking Strategy decide they must aim to please the dominator. Can you imagine the mental and physical energy consumed by all this stroking? But people are willing to spend it when driven by fear. If subordinates who are operating out of fear sense they have stepped on an eggshell, or danced the wrong dance, they just know their heads will roll. The only defense, the only leverage they can use in these situations is to point to all their pleasing behaviors. They can use all their Stroking Strategies to argue to the dominator that they do not deserve any hurt/shame/attack.

Before Debbie would leave the house, she made sure everything was fixed for the family—dinner in the oven, pajamas out for the kids, clean towels, etc. She was careful never to inconvenience John—even though John enjoyed cooking, and liked getting the children ready for bed. She expected nothing of her husband, does everything herself, and internalized the resentment and fear for years. How can Debbie learn to relate to her husband without stroking? Without fear? Without expectation of attack?

Fortunately, the safety of the therapeutic setting allowed Debbie to work past the pain in her relationship with her father, and become able to trust and love John the way she really wanted and needed to—in safety. Now, if Debbie makes an honest mistake, she does not fear retaliation and does not go into a panic attack.

THE SUBMISSION STRATEGY

In the Submission Strategy, the subordinate person *gives up his/her power* and allows the dominator to use his/her power to control. The rationale is that if the dominator feels powerful enough, if the dominator gets everything his/her way, then the subordinate will be safe. The trade off is power for safety.

The process of the Submission Strategy is:

1. Determine where and how the dominator likes to be powerful.

2. Give up power over one's self and life.

Goal: With the dominator feeling powerful, he/she will be happy and there will be no abuse/oppression, and life will be safe.

It is unfortunate that when one human being has power over another, the dominator usually uses it for selfish, ego-centered purposes, for their own comfort. History is replete with examples of one group overpowering another to satisfy their own greed, needs, ego—slavery in the U.S. and other countries, genocides, Hitler, Crusades, Spanish Inquisition, and many, many more. When the dominators use God or religion to justify the domination it makes it especially difficult to confront them or for them to change their behaviors—they justify their oppression of others.

The same thing can happen on the micro level. It can be seen in parental abuse/neglect of children; of a boss not providing safety equipment for workers; domestic violence, etc. Or, it can be seen in more subtle forms of oppression such as giving women tranquilizers instead of medical tests; unwritten rules about limiting the levels of promotion for certain minority groups; or just the patronizing grin or the rolling of the eyes that says the subordinate is not to be taken seriously. Sometimes subordinates, in order to avoid feeling helpless, may rationalize that the oppressive use of power is acceptable as "God's will" for them. They may use Scripture or religious teachings to convince themselves that they will be rewarded for the obeisance. When one's safety is at stake, and submission appears to be the only way to make one's world safe, a person will do it, for whatever reasons, and use whatever reasons, rationalizations, minimizing, etc., to distance the terrible helplessness it generates.

Sheila was confused. She was pregnant for the second time. Ever since the first baby was born, Edward was jealous and demanding. No matter what Sheila did, it was never enough to please him. Edward's possessiveness progressed to the point of relocating their family far away from Sheila's family and friends (and childcare resources), to taking over the checkbook, and to giving her a meager allowance. He would not fix her car, so she could only go out with him. Edward wanted every niche of power he could get. One night Edward burst into a fit of anger, pushed Sheila, threatening the pregnancy and her physical safety. She took their little girl by the hand and walked out the front door. If it were not for the local women's shelter, Sheila would have had no place to go.

While in the shelter, Sheila contacted her pastor for counsel. The pastor felt it was clear that Sheila was not meeting Edward's needs adequately. It was Edward's place to be the "head" of the home, to be in control. What Edward wants is what Sheila should do. If Sheila would just submit more, Edward would ease his threatening behavior. He quoted Ephesians about how Christian women are instructed to submit, and God would reward her if she did not insist on her own way. Sheila returned home (against the advice of the shelter), committed to do what she was told—give more power to Edward. Three weeks later, Sheila, the fetus and the daughter were dead. And Edward shot himself as well. Submitting may make the world safer temporarily, but it only reinforces the dominator's insatiable lust for power.

Is it possible to follow Scriptural or religious guidelines for "submission" without jeopardizing security? Without enabling the oppressive use of power? Without teaching the dominator that it is acceptable to use power for selfish needs? Could Sheila have submitted and be safe?

Submission must meet two conditions to be positive, healthy:

1. Submission is VOLUNTARY. When submission is demanded, then it is oppression (slavery). When submission is voluntary, it is usually a response to love and caring. For an example from religion, when a person sees the love and sacrifice of Christ on the cross, to submit to it is almost automatic and compelling. When parents demonstrate love and protection for their children, when the children's needs are more important than their own, the chil-

dren feel safe. When a company puts worker safety and needs above profits, they will have loyal workers.

2. Submission should result in the GOOD of everyone. If submitting means that one's values are violated, sense of self is compromised, then it is not submission—it is intimidation. When submission means that everyone wins, problems are solved, everyone benefits, and then it is truly healthy submission. The negotiation, compromise or bargaining involved does not humiliate or degrade anyone involved.

Contrast this with the destructive side of submission. When one submits only to avoid fear, the dynamics of submission are completely different. When a woman or man submits to avoid pain, he/she pushes himself/herself deeper and deeper into a state of helplessness and powerlessness. It produces no greater good. Submitting to someone's ego, narcissism, addiction, need for power, or perversion is NOT a greater good. It is of no value to the dominator or the subordinate. Sheila's submission only created more fear and, ultimately death.

Many people in relationships that are originally loving or caring may submit out of good intentions. They want to make the other person happy, keep peace, and have events turn out nice. The anticipation is that these efforts would be met with appreciation and maybe even reciprocated. But all too often, when the partner has power or ego needs, these efforts are not appreciated. The dominator instead expects more giving in, more submission. The submission ended up reinforcing the narcissism rather than generating a closer, more bonded relationship. There was no way of knowing this in the beginning—she/he was just sincerely trying out of a loving heart to make things better, but it didn't.

People in Sheila's position often say things like:

"I can't."

"I'm afraid to..."

"I just don't know what to do."

You can hear the paralysis in these statements. After years of destructive submission, a beaten-down person is unable to take action for one's self. The subordinate is totally immobilized when left on his/her own. A woman such as Sheila cannot begin to confront the tremendous anger that results from the victim role. With increased submission comes increased fear.

I have seen the horrible damage which is done to Christian or Muslim women who have submitted and submitted again thinking and believing that this was the will of God. They have been honest, sincere and absolute in their desire to do what they think God wants them to do, but they have been deceived by teachings that say that self-destructive submission is God's will. Why should God's will hurt so much? For what purpose? To teach a power-hungry, mean dominator that he/she is entitled to their way? Many browbeaten people never get to a therapist, and those who do are defeated, numb, severely lacking in a sense of self. To take action on their own behalf is unthinkable. Therapists need to respect the courage it takes for these people to even go to counseling, and to not push too fast or too hard to get them to take action for themselves. Therapists need to respect the size of the fear that has created the problem and work with it gently.

These hurting men and women are sitting next to us in church, in the cube next to us at work, down the street in our neighborhood. Children, both young and older, often have been convinced that oppression is justified when it is at the hands of parents, since, after all, one must honor one's parents. This is a confusing message—does honoring one's parents include being abused, humiliated, shamed, etc? Here, again, the principle that submission should result in greater good of everyone needs to be applied.

THE SEX STRATEGY

This is probably the oldest of all strategies. Women, and in some situations, men also, have learned to *give sexual favors* to keep the dominator happy and obtain a safe place for themselves. This wrong has been perpetrated throughout history.

The simple step of the Sex Strategy is this (and there is only one step this time):

1. When the dominator wants sexual gratification, give it.

Goal: When the dominator is sexually gratified, your world will be safer.

Even if the dominator in some areas of business is female, it has been reported that sexual favors have been requested of male subordinates in return for promotions, leave time, etc. Sometimes sex is used not just to gain a favor but to not lose what they already have, or to avoid punishment.

I have worked in a domestic violence shelter and a women's substance abuse program in the Detroit area. It is common for these women to submit to sex to get what they need for every-day existence. Most of them are inner city women who have nothing so sex is exchanged for food and shelter. But women in wealthier situations may not always be better off. I have heard stories of how they have exchanged sex for peace the next day, for extra money for the children's sports costs, to not be hit, to get him to be courteous at the family gathering, etc.

Money and status makes little difference when one is in the dominator/subordinate system, when one is afraid, and sex is the only leverage available.

The Sex Strategy can also work indirectly. Allie worked for a boss who was having an affair with one of her female coworkers. The boss was married and so was the coworker. The boss and the coworker went to lunch together and often stayed away for two or three hours. In the meantime, Allie had to work doubly hard to make sure everything was done at the end of the day. This made Allie very angry. She felt the boss was using her indirectly for his sexual indulgences. However, Allie feared to confront him or the coworker about it—she could lose her job, and there are not many jobs to be had in her city. Covering up for the affair made Allie feel like a victim of their sexual behavior.

The most extreme picture of the sex strategy between a dominator and a subordinate is incest. A child (powerless, helpless, who needs the protection of the adult) cannot protest against the very one who provides his/her daily needs. Many of the boy and girl victims, when they reach adulthood continue this intense feeling of helplessness and fear. Even as adults, they perceive other adults as having tremendous power over them, and see themselves as having little control over themselves. In other words, the child sexual abuse role was so stamped into their little minds and bodies that the fact that they are grown up does not matter. They still fear anyone that 5% reminds them of the perpetrator. It is the ultimate misuse of power. It is the ultimate living in fear generated from within (what should be) a loving relationship.

If at a young age, these helpless children learn that the only way to receive affection, shelter, avoid hurt, is to exchange sex for it, that is what they will do. They see few options. The dominator who supplies their daily needs is too big and too powerful to resist. Usually in therapy with incest survivors, it is common to see that the incest continued until a time when the victim gained some sense of power—that they could physically fight back, had the verbal power to stop the abuse, could run away, or were able to engage another powerful person to protect them. Can they find/tap this instinctive power of survival for themselves today?

I have worked with female patients whose previous male therapist demanded sex. I have worked with women whose male pastors took advantage of them sexually. Somehow males who are sexually demanding find females with incest histories as easy objects. All of these women feared males, feared to verbalize their anger against them, feared to enforce boundaries with them (which, by the way, it is the ethical requirement of the authority figure to enforce the safety of the patient/client, etc.) and would not report them for fear it would bring retaliation or the humiliation of not being believed. When the adults around them did not protect them from sexual abuse, or when they were not believed, or when the only way to avoid harm was to give in sexually, they learned important lessons about their self esteem, their bodies and their integrity—it isn't worth much! Undoing that in adulthood is difficult. That childhood image makes them vulnerable to abusive dominators in adulthood.

The tragedy of using sex for safety is that the potential for sex to be a source of intimacy and joy is lost. The pleasure that was designed for us to experience during sex is destroyed. Often men or women involved in the Sex Strategy say, "I feel like a piece of meat." Think of the additional helplessness and ambivalence when pregnancy results from these sexual experiences. What was intended to create intimacy and joy only generates fear and victimization.

THE SCHOLARSHIP STRATEGY

This section could be called, "Subordinates who read too much and the dominators who have to live with them." The goal is—*learn everything you can* about the dominator, either by guessing, reading, observing, etc. For example, self help books are purchased and read by the thousands—mostly subordinates. While the dominators have life the way they like it, the oppressed are crying for help and will find it anywhere they can. *The only way a subordinate can truly know the thoughts, feelings and motives of the dominator, is for the dominator to communicate them.* But dominators know that NOT communicating their agenda is a powerful method for keeping subordinates helpless and squirming. So those who are left living in fear must resort to guessing, reading, wondering, etc.

The Scholarship Strategy follows this pattern:

1. The subordinate knows there are problems, but the dominant person denies them.

2. The subordinate seeks out books, pre-planning, filling in the blanks, to help "get into the head" of the dominator, thinking they can figure him/her out.

Goal: By applying the information in the books (or other sources), the subordinate feels more enabled and in control and less fearful.

If the subordinate, fearful person can learn about the dominator from books, from some outside sources, from Dr. Phil, or by mentally writing scripts which play out what they think may happen, there is an illusion (key work, "illusion") that he/she can plan a strategy to make their world safer, to reduce the fear. Since the life of the oppressed person is impacted so strongly by the dominator, he/she will want to know as much as possible about what makes the dominator tick. Knowledge is power, and the person living in fear needs all the power (knowledge) available—whether it is from books, or from obsessive observation, or whatever.

Literature about the days of slavery gives examples of the Scholarship Strategy. We read how the slaves studied the moves, moods, and minds of their masters to learn what they do, where, how and when. Slaves who worked in the master's house were an invaluable source of such information. They had access to "inside information." As they shared this knowledge with other slaves, the slaves could plan their secret meetings, ways to escape, or hide to avoid being raped or beaten.

The survivors of the holocaust used the same Scholarship Strategy. They microscopically observed the timing and systems of the Nazi officers in order to know when they were safe to move about and talk. They had been robbed of all personal dignity and this was one way of regaining some control over their lives. Living in fear compels people to do whatever they can to hold on to some sense of control. If one is afraid and does not know the "temperature" of the dominator, several options can be used:

- Remain in the dark, risk uncertainty, suffer tension and prepare for the unpredictable.

- Try to guess what the dominator might be thinking/doing and plan accordingly, except those guesses are usually wrong.

- Revert to outside sources (books, etc.) to learn about the dominator, and make changes based on the information.

Consider the first option—remain in the dark. When one is living in fear that is generated from within a relationship, ignorance is not bliss. Remaining in the dark leaves the subordinate feeling like a cork floating on rapids—chaotic and out of control. To bounce around day after day, not knowing what will happen, fills the life of the subordinate with stress and apprehension. Having your life pivot around an unpredictable, unsafe person is terrifying.

The second option is adopted when the mind is put to use to feel more control. I say, "feel more control" because, in actuality, one has no more control than before all the guessing. What the subordinate does is to try to figure out the whole game of checkers in his/her mind—then all the counter moves can be anticipated and the subordinate can plan for how to keep from losing. People feel that if they can anticipate oncoming attacks or problems, one can prepare for them, which is the definition of *worry*. The only problem is that a person can pre-plan 500 different scenarios and none of them may happen—but their minds and emotions are completely worn out and they have lost a lot of sleep. Why doesn't this work? Because no one can really anticipate how the game will go, and all the preplanning is wasted. As soon as the dominator pulls a move that was not anticipated, things are out of control again. To try to preplan every possible move leaves one exhausted mentally and emotionally. The preplanning can, actually, exacerbate the helplessness that the subordinate already feels.

James is an example of someone who uses option two. James is a very shy fellow, fearful of authority figures. If James' boss just looks at him the wrong way, he shudders. His new boss wanted to build a team approach, so the boss asked each worker to make a presentation of how individual jobs interplay with others. James called me within minutes of the announcement. He was petrified! He could not possibly speak in front of his boss.

During our session, James went on and on with a host of guesses about what could happen to him—embarrassment, humiliation, disapproval, anguish, make a fool of himself, freeze in front of everyone, be fired, and other worst possible outcomes. Such anxiety happens when one's safety and future is dependent on a powerful person's approval, and when one such as James feels he can never gain it. He was expending much time and energy in generating possibilities that may never happen. James believed, as many fearful subordinates do, that if he could plan for every possibility, he would be safe. The only problem is—it doesn't work, will only wear James out and each plan will only make the boss seem scarier. The more James inflated his fear with worry, the more he was creating a monster of his boss, making him even more powerful, creating a vicious cycle. Whenever we run from anything, we make it bigger.

The same time and energy could be spent on preparing the presentation and practicing it, i.e., focusing on what James CAN do. Besides, I pointed out, no one ever knows positively what another's response will be until it happens. Wait and find out what the response to his presentation will be with the assurance (lots of assurance) that should it be negative, then we will work on how to cope with it. I tried to help James focus on his adult role, to remember times past when similar projects went well, and to project that this will go well too. We worked on bringing the boss "down to size". We concentrated on the choices that *were realistic* and how they could help him feel more control. James finally decided to use several power point diagrams to outline his job—it would put the audience focus on the charts instead of on him.

Even if we know someone well enough to possibly predict behavior, it is impossible to score 100%. No one can read another's mind. Guessing is ultimately self-defeating. But for those caught in the Scholarship Strategy, when the dominant, fear-inducing other does not communicate, is unpredictable or feared because of past experiences (with that person or similar persons), then guessing and preplanning is a common response. It makes the subordinates feel they are *doing something* but in the end it is a waste of energy.

The third option listed above is to learn about the dominant from outside sources—books, seminars, professionals, classes, etc. It the dominant won't talk then find out about him/her from somewhere/someone else who might know. Learn how the dominant person ticks, then the subordinate can manipulate hopefully with success to end the fear and regain safety.

One man, who felt oppressed and frustrated in his marriage, came to my office and on the first visit actually said, "I will tell you about my wife and I want you to tell me know I can change her." He was applying the Scholarship Strategy to handle his own powerlessness. He sought out a professional female who (he thought) could tell him what he needed to know with the anticipation that he would have tools to use to change her (to be less afraid of her). I can appreciate the helplessness of a subordinate person, but trying to analyze a person without his/her actual data is fruitless and disrespectful. Even if the subordinate person learns, assumes, guesses the motives, thoughts, and feelings of the dominant person, in the end the subordinate still does not really KNOW anything unless the dominant person confirms it.

In order to not get caught in this cycle that is the inevitable result of the Scholarship Strategy, the subordinate must learn to "leave the blanks empty" and wait until the dominant person fills in the data. As each adult expresses his/her own thoughts and feelings whenever he/she chooses to do so, only then will the subordinate accurately know what is in the other person's mind, and only than can the subordinate accurately respond. They must play checkers making one move at a time, waiting and allowing for the other to choose his/her move in return. If the other person chooses to not communicate their thoughts and feelings, and perhaps passively/aggressively (which is a power play) withholds, then one needs to decide whether to be controlled by this.

There are two rules for adult relationships: 1) We only know what the other person tells us; 2) We are not responsible for what they do not tell us. What relief! Granted, when one lives with an unpredictable, fear-inducing person, and that person does not communicate, it is quite uncomfortable. But these rules spare the subordinate the worry, preplanning, assuming, mind guessing, etc., that only wears and weakens the subordinate. Rule number two relieves the subordinate of the responsibility of trying to figure out the dominant. The time and energy can then be spent on being connected with one's self, sorting what is/isn't within one's control, planning what is possible, and learning ways to keep one's self safe.

From a therapists point of view, it can be easy to let the patient be focused on the dominant person, or to join in on the guessing game of what they think is going on in his/her head, or what they expect the dominant person will do when…., or making assumptions about motives, etc. If the Scholarship Strategy is operating, it is important to let the patient vent as much as needed, but then to direct the focus to the patient, and to see the fruitlessness of the assuming and guessing, how infantilizing it is, and how it actually makes him/her feel even more helpless. Pointing out the two rules of adult behavior (above) is useful to draw energy away from the Scholarship Strategy.

SUMMARY

Here is a quick review of the strategies:

The Sacrifice Strategy—the subordinate sets aside his/her own needs to fully meet the needs of the dominator. Please the powerful person so he/she will have no reason to be angry, or do anything that would threaten the subordinate's safety.

The Suppression Strategy—avoid sharing opinions or feelings with which the dominator disagrees to avoid disapproval or anything that would make the subordinate's world unsafe.

The Stroking Strategy—to earn brownie points, and when there is trouble, the subordinate can "cash in" the points to be safer.

The Submission Strategy—where the subordinate person gives up his/her power and allows the dominator to use his/her power to control, thinking that if the dominator has the control he/she wants, then the subordinate will be safe.

The Sex Strategy—give sexual favors to keep the dominator happy and in good spirits and thereby keep safe.

<u>The Scholarship Strategy</u>—read everything possible, ask experts, find information to make the subordinate feel that the have the knowledge to predict, assume, plan what the dominator needs, do it, and then everything will be safer.

Each of the strategies discussed here is ultimately self-destructive, each in its own way. Helplessness and prolonged fear generated within a previous caring or loving relationship inevitably leads to some type(s) of strategy to be safe, because *safety is a primary, basic need.* But each of these strategies only leads to feeling more helpless, more afraid, and less safe ultimately. The aim of each strategy is to be a better scale balancer. It cannot be done. One person cannot make a safe relationship.

The sign that a strategy is not working is when it is not reducing fear adequately in the long run. And none of these strategies do. They are short-term ideas that seem to win the current "battle" but ultimately lose the war. Adapting to fear in any manner is always a losing proposition. Aside from being in a prison camp, there are options.

It is good to know what *does not* work to provide motivation for what can work better.

Wouldn't it be wonderful if relationships could be set free from fear before they ended up in divorce? Before people hurt each other so much that repair isn't possible? Before Sheila died? Before James moves from job to job? Before people develop debilitating or terminal illnesses?

3

EMPOWERMENT

It was a hot summer afternoon in Fresno, California, as several hundred women filtered into a convention arena. Sixty people headed for a workshop entitled, "You Can't Be Powerful if You're Afraid." As the presenter, I shared the essence of Section I (what fear is and the problem of prolonged fear generated from within relationships) and Section II (the self-destructive strategies for dealing with fear). Heads nodded in confirmation, with comments such as, "You've just explained the story of my life."

The inevitable question arose," What do we do now?" "Where do we go from here?" I asked someone to do a role-play with me. We wanted to re-create the feeling of someone caught in a relationship where prolonged fear entered in. Roberta volunteered. She sat on the floor in front of me, and made herself as "small" as possible, to enact the fear. I stood on a chair and loomed over her, making myself as "big" as possible, speaking and behaving in an intimidating manner. After the scenario was sufficiently created, I asked her,

"How do you feel?" I looked down at her.

"Small, scared, helpless," she answered.

"How do you like this arrangement?" I asked.

"I don't," replied Roberta. "It's awful."

"How long are you willing to stay down there?" I inquired.

"Hmmm. I hope for not long. I want out but I'm not sure what to do to get out."

"How can YOU change the situation?" I challenged.

Roberta thought for a moment. She looked up at me and pleaded, "You could stop making me afraid."

P.S.—it never hurts to find out if a fear-inducing person is willing to back away. However, the rule-of-thumb is that people who abuse power rarely give it up willingly. "No," I said.

When someone lives in a fearful situation, the tendency is to focus on the oppressor, to figure out how to change him/her (Section II). So I dropped a hint to Roberta, and asked again, "What can YOU do to change the situation?"

Roberta looked up at me again, "What can *I* do?"

"Yes, what can YOU do?"

She thought. The first time a subordinate shifts the focus off the oppressor and onto herself it usually takes a little time to adjust to this revolutionary idea.

I guided Roberta further. "Yes, what can YOU do to lift yourself up?"

"To lift MYSELF up?" she repeated.

Roberta, now inspired with permission to think beyond old limits, and with about 60 cheerleaders behind her, looked around the room. She reached out to the people sitting on either side of her, and asked, "Will you help lift me up?"

STARTING THE EMPOWERMENT PROCESS

Let's review the role-play and "freeze frame" some of the moments for the sake of analysis. Each step has much to tell us.

DETERMINE THE GAP

The place to start is to determine, realistically, to what extent prolonged fear has changed the relationship. How "small" have you become? How "big" has the feared person become? In many instances, because we work or live in the situation daily, we will deny the degree of fear, rationalize the actions of the dominator, not be aware of how slowly and insidiously the fear has crept in. It is said that if you put a frog in a pot of boiling water, it will jump out. But if you put a frog into a pot of cold water, and slowly raise the heat, it will stay in and eventually die. This is an accurate metaphor for relationships that start off fine, caring, loving, safe, hopeful, then one party slowly raises the fear ("heat") level. In the same gradual way, one or more of the strategies is employed to handle it, to keep things safe, balanced. But at some point, if the subordinate stays in the "pot" he/she will die—maybe not physically (although sometimes this happens), but at least emotionally, and the sense of self dies too. We need to determine how "hot" the situation is, what is the power gap, what is the urgency?

An attorney friend of mine handled some divorce cases where the women had been verbally, emotionally and/or physically beaten down during many years of destructive marriages. He asked me, "How could these women become so afraid, so lost? It is clear they are intelligent, reasonable women?" My answer was in the form of a question, "If I came into your office every morning and sanded an imperceptible amount of wood from the legs of your chair, when would you notice it was shorter?" He nodded in understanding.

It is painful, sometimes shameful, to admit fear. It forces one to accept a reality one does not want to admit. If I love someone, it is hard to admit the truth that he/she has become oppressive and controlling and that fear is there. It causes emotions that collide with love. At what point does fear overtake love? When does one more weed squeeze out the flowers?

When one determines the gap truthfully, it may preclude change. Should that change be too threatening—quitting a job, a divorce, a family split, etc., then the denial of the fear protects one from making the obvious change. In short, for example, if financial difficulty is feared more than an abusive marriage, she will stay and deny the fear. This does NOT mean she condones it, but rather that, unconsciously, she will minimize or rationalize the fear in order to avoid a scary change.

Roberta was readily able to tell us she felt weak, afraid and helpless. When one feels "small" in relation to a "big" other person, it may not be so easy to answer the question, "How do you feel?" However, unless the gap is accurately determined, the options are lost.

There are three great motivators of change—when one is afraid enough, when one is scared enough, when one is angry enough. Overcoming denial and admitting the "enough" of fear may take time and a safe setting to do. Roberta looked around the room and saw people who would listen and be honest with her.

Perhaps a letter I received in response to my first book, Hiding, Hurting, Healing (Zondervan Press, 1985) can best exemplify the "determining the gap".

> The book spoke to me because it was objective and didn't lead me to place blame but helped me understand the oppression I feel. I am the daughter of an abusive, alcoholic father, and have been married five years and feeling pretty low. I love my husband very much. He's interested in me when it comes to meeting his needs and his expectations. I feel like a dog always trying to please him, jumping through hoops, and when I get close to doing right, he jerks the hoops so that I can never measure up. My needs and feelings seldom enter the scene if I try to share them. He punishes me by rejection or turning things around until I'm so confused.

I talked to two older godly women. They keep hitting me over the head with submit and that I'm responsible for not making the hoops. I've written (to major radio/television Christian ministers) and all of them tell me submit, sumit, submit. I have submitted myself to the point of spiritual and emotional death. I know now that I can only change myself. How do I make the positive changes without reaping the overwhelming rejection of my husband? Needless to tell you, my self-esteem has gone through the floor, I am unhappy and if my husband senses it, he withdraws. I want a life that my husband respects, accepts and loves but mainly one that I can live and be free without fear, anger and oppression.

Please help.

You wouldn't believe how good it feels to write to you knowing that my life is important. I used to feel that it was important. To write for help from someone who sees me and my life as important is helping me to believe that again.

—Lynn, Tennessee

From this letter one can see the results of power inequality—helplessness, feeling "small," afraid. Lynn herself admits she has submitted to the point of emotional and spiritual death. How much smaller can one become? No one has helped Lynn "determine the gap" and she wrote to me hoping I would. She reached out to me like Roberta reached out to the women in the conference room. A subordinate may be able to determine the gap on his/her own, but more often it helps to have a caring, honest outsider (professional or friend) to help with the assessment.

STRONG MODELS

Lynn's letter was an attempt to reach out to a model—someone she looked up to, felt was strong, caring and empathic. The fact that she had to write to an out-of-state author makes me all the more aware of how few models are readily available, particularly to abused women whose husbands tend to isolate them. Especially within religious communities, there tends to be a lack of strong women models. It is a shame especially in light of how many strong women are mentioned in the Old and New Testaments. Jesus encountered many "small" women—a Samaritan woman who had five husbands, a prostitute, a woman caught in adultery, a bent-over woman, a hemorrhaging woman, etc.—and he made them strong! If Lynn could only talk to one of these women, she would get very good advice. Dr. Mary Stewart VanLeeuwen states it succinctly in her book, Gender and Grace (Intervarsity Press, 1989, p. 154):

And while I wish I could say that churches are in the vanguard of those helping women "grow up" into healthy balance of altruism and independence, I know that this is often not the case. Too many churches discourage independent thought and leadership in women as being unfeminine or unsubmissive. Too many respond with pity for single women who lack husbands to "look after" them—as if a woman supporting herself in an extra-domestic calling were somehow a breach of the creation order. And the fact that some women use church order as an excuse not to exercise independent thought and action does not make this practice any more laudable. It rather suggests that neither sex has acknowledged the fallenness of such behavior, the way it has been inflated by gender role socialization and the way in which it is perpetuated by unjust social structures that leave women so few options for action.

The religious teachings often give men permission to rule over women and it also teaches women that this is the way it is destined to be by God. This leaves few options for women to seek and exercise strength, and leaves few options for men to see and value women as strong. Men and women need to see other men and women who have power but who do not use it to abuse or to serve their egos. Power is like nuclear energy—it can be used to make bombs or it can be used to light a city. There are "models" who demonstrate one or the other.

The business community has improved in its value and affirmation of women, but the "glass ceiling" is still all too familiar. Men still too often guard their power and use their old boy's network to protect it. There is a woman I know in a major corporation who has had the burden of being the "first female" for many years—she has been the first woman to have many of the positions to which she has been promoted. She has been the pioneer to forge the way for other women, and it has NOT been easy. She feels she needed to prove her capabilities at each step of the way, every day, and the men in charge have tested her sometimes mercilessly. Again, those who hold power rarely give it up to anyone other than their "in-group" without kicking and screaming.

FLEXING OUR MUSCLES

It would be foolish for a boxer to go into a ring to face an opponent who is much larger, stronger and more powerful. Before the boxer would even consider taking on such a match, he/she would take time out to lift weights, run, exercise, get into shape. The boxer does not need to out-size the opponent. He/she only needs to build up enough muscle to gain a fighting chance. Any person who finds himself/herself in a "small" state needs to do exactly the same thing—find a place, a trainer, a sparring partner, whatever is available to begin the process of strengthening the weak areas.

People who live in the love/fear dilemma live with symptoms mentioned in Section One—it makes them tired, weak, oppressed. They need to be strengthened. Roberta needs to find ways to make herself stronger to deal with her (role-play) oppressor, to help her stand on her feet, which would reduce the gap between her and the oppressor. She needs to stop looking at how strong and powerful the oppressor is, and start to focus on how much stronger and more powerful SHE can become!

The misuse of power is hurting many people in our world. The conflicts in Iraq depict this on the global level; domestic violence depicts this on the local level. Oppression anywhere means that people are not safe. Lynn deserves a fighting chance to be strong, to be her self, to be a person utilizing all her talents and abilities. She deserves to be free, happy and safe. If her husband denies this to her, she must find ways to find it for herself (as is true for all adults).

In the business community, agencies such as the Equal Employment Opportunity Commission (EEOC) was established to give women and minorities more "muscle" to deal with employers who denied them safe work places, or denied them opportunities for hiring and promotion in a fair manner. However, the number of cases brought to the EEOC versus the ones settled in favor of the victims is low. In addition, companies can violate any of the EEO laws anytime they want—it is up to the injured party to file the case, produce "enough" evidence and protect him/herself. The oppressed person is required to speak up for himself/herself—not always an easy thing to do especially when the odds of a just outcome are low.

When I shared the Fresno story of our role-play with Gail back in my office, she winced at the word "power". Even though she too was in a "small" victim role in her own life, the idea of having power was repulsive. Why? Because the only powerful person Gail ever knew was her cruel, insensitive grandmother. Even her own mother was afraid of Grandmom's presence. Gail talked about Grandmom's verbal ability to "slice her down the middle" so quickly she never even saw Grandmom draw the "knife"! Her vicious tongue had no competition in the county. Grandmom could humiliate Gail to the point where she would hide in terror. Today, does Gail want power? No. The only definition of power that Gail understood was that it is something used to hurt and create fear in others. Grandmom used her power to make "bombs". Even though Grandmom faithfully attended the local church every Sunday, the only behavior Gail saw at home was quite unloving. What a contradiction.

In reality, power is the medicine for fear. But it must be clear that it is NOT power OVER others that solves the fear/safety dilemma. The answer is not for Gail to "slice up" Grandmom worse than Grandmom "sliced up" her. The solution is for Gail to have the power to defend, protect and free herself.

The power that Roberta needs is to flex her emotional muscle, not so that she can intimidate her oppressor back. Rather, the goal for Roberta is to become stronger within herself so that it is impossible for anyone to intimidate her. She needs to feel that her self-power is equal to that of others in her world. She needs to learn to be an equal sparring partner to any "big" person who comes against her. One does not lift up by beating the other person down. The "big" person comes down automatically as one becomes stronger and lifts him/herself up. When one feels inwardly strong, the foe is not so formidable.

BOUNDARIES

Strength can be developed from the adaptation and implementation of appropriate boundaries. When people feel fearful, one usually finds instances where oppressors have routinely violated boundaries. In the beginning the relationship may been respectful and caring, but later one party began violating boundaries, bringing fear into the relationship.

For example, later in their relationship her husband always told Lynn that she was wrong. Gail's dignity was attacked by Grandmom. Look back to other examples used throughout Section II and you will see many violations of boundaries. When others violate our person, respect, integrity, bodies, self-esteem, identity, self-control, opinions, feelings, intelligence, etc., then boundaries have been overstepped. When what is rightly ours is attacked by a "big" person, and we don't have the tools to protect ourselves, then fear sets in and we get "small."

When discussing boundaries, I often ask a patient to picture a back yard like yards in suburban areas—no fences. A neighbor, who used to be friendly and nice, one day throws garbage into your yard. I ask, "What do you do when garbage is thrown into your yard?" The answers I receive vary.

- Stand on my porch and cry.

- Scream at the dumping person.

- Retreat to my house and eat, drink, have sex, clean, gamble, etc. (use addictions), to feel better.

- Fantasize.

- Become physically sick, then the neighbor will feel sorry for me and stop.

- Take out my anger on an innocent party who won't hurt me back.

- Take care of the garbage and be co-dependent.

- Give up on my yard and let the garbage pile up.

- Resent the garbage and seethe silently.

My next question is, "What can you do to protect your yard?" Before this can be answered, one must establish the belief that this is YOUR yard. When people have been afraid for a long time, they forget they are the owners of their emotional and physical selves. The yard belongs to them! Ownership must be clearly established.

The next step is HOW to protect one's yard. The first idea that comes to mind is to build a fence. Usually, the way to protect one's yard and at the same time try to not offend anyone would be to put up a cute, little picket fence. It would be pretty, hopefully get the message across, and perhaps solve the problem. So here comes the nasty neighbor again and easily tosses the garage up and over the little fence.

Now what? You guessed it—a bigger, higher fence, one that gives a clearer message and works better. Here is where new emotional muscles are tested. This is now a critical point of protection. The larger fence is up; the feared neighbor has arrived. He/she is angry at the bigger fence, presses against it, threatens and rages. He/she cannot throw the garbage over. How dare you not allow him/her to throw garbage in your yard? Can you keep the fence up in spite of the anger and threat? If a person backs down at this time, the garbage will keep coming. What is sad is that originally everyone liked each other and there were no problems and it was delightful to walk in and out of each other's yards. No one ever thought about a fence, until one day one person violated the respect and integrity of another's yard.

Martha was in a physically and emotionally abusive marriage. It took about a year to start exercising her muscle, and to believe that she had the right to protect herself. Naturally, the husband resisted. The stronger she became, the more he threatened. But she continued to take control and keep her "fence" to guard her body and emotions. One day her husband threatened to "flatten her out on the floor." Her response was, "If you do, I will get up and call the police and don't think I won't." There is no other way to stop fear-inducing behavior than with strength.

It is important to see that all the fear/love interactions described in Section II were attempts to sooth or manipulate the feared person into not violating our yards any further. The goal is logical, but the methods in Section II did not work. It only gave the oppressor more opportunity to dominate more. The more the strategies were used, the more helpless and victimized the subordinate felt. They thought they were protecting their yards, but none of the methods achieved this goal.

There have been many excellent books on boundaries in the self-help market in the past years—any one of them will be helpful to learn the specifics of "fence building". The bottom line is that no one will love or care for us if we allow them to be disrespectful of us (throw garbage into our yards). We need to establish respect first—respect for ourselves, and respect in our relationships—and boundaries are the respect builders. Boundaries require assertiveness (not aggression, not passivity). Again, we need to be prepared and be consistent when/if the oppressor objects, dislikes, and is angry about the boundaries. If one stays consistent with boundaries, either the neighbor will regain his/her respect for you and the relationship will thrive again, or, the neighbor will find some other yard in which to throw garbage. Either way, you are safer, stronger and happier.

SUPPORT SYSTEMS

Finally, one of Roberta's efforts to help herself lift up from her "small" position was to look for people around her who could help lift her up. The whole concept of support groups has certainly swelled in the past decades—there is an "A" group for just about anything. These groups supply the hands that one needs to grasp when your own are too weak. It is a wise and courageous adult who reaches out when help is needed.

Before the invention of the automobile, when communities were not mobile, families grew up and lived within a mile or so of each other. No one was ever isolated. When there was an illness, other families took care of the children and brought over food. When a new baby was born, the neighbors took over household chores and helped with the baby so the mother could rest. Everyone was an agent of comfort in the face of death. Neighborhoods and extended families were available support systems. But now, with the corporate mentality of IBM (I've Been Moved), often there are no long-standing contacts in one's arena of living. A new mom has no support. A depressed man has no one to talk to. A scared teen is alone. Isolation was not the way we were meant to live. Support systems are not optional—they are necessary. Some controllers, oppressors, purposely isolate their victims to have more power over them by moving them away from support systems. Husbands may move their families away from the wife's friends and families; the employer may place an employee in a nearby cube to make sure he/she does not talk with certain other people. Being afraid AND alone is overwhelming. But it is probably just what the dominant person wants.

Communities do not offer as many opportunities for building support systems as they used to. Some neighborhoods create a "community" but many do not. One can make contacts around the schools if they have children in school; community interest groups; churches; music/art organizations, etc. But these are not automatically available—one must go out and take the time to mix and meet in order to make friends. It takes time to build trust before one can go to them with some of the more vulnerable issues one might be experiencing—the issues that generate fear.

So Roberta reached out to the people in the workshop who had strength and were willing to lend it to her until she became strong. Lynn's letter reached out to find someone from whom she could share strength until she became stronger. Support systems are the medicine of isolation and fear.

INNER STRENGTH AS EMPOWERMENT

Even with the good fortune of a support system, the "small" person may need to engage in therapy to learn how the "small" image/role was imbedded, perhaps early in life. How did fear start? What caused it to continue?

The old proverb says, "Give a person a fish, and he/she will eat today; teach a person to fish, he/she will eat for a lifetime." Roberta may end up leaving her feared person, James may change jobs, etc. However, the "feared person" in one's life is bound to show up in another form in another place at another time. Quitting the job, divorce, changing churches, etc., is not always the answer. On the other hand, *there are times when leaving is the wisest thing to do.* But even then it is still essential to alter the "small" role to deal with controllers and unsafe people in the future. There are not many of these in the world, but they are out there, and dealing with them is an essential skill. One will not fear going out into any area of the world if he/she knows how to protect and empower one's self.

It is helpful to understand fear, how fear effects individuals, their history with fear, when and where they may expect to be afraid, how they developed responses to fear. These are keys to having power over fear in the future. To feel like a confident, empowered adult, it is worth the time to explore those who were feared in childhood, analyze the characteristics of the feared person, what were the "messages" from the feared person (that may still be playing in our heads), what coping skills they may have tried to use, etc. Then with the assistance of the therapist, they can identify triggers, learn alternate coping skills, set boundaries, etc.

STEP ONE: VALIDATE REALITY AND FEELINGS

Two of the key elements in empowerment are to validate one's reality and validate one's feelings. Among the many characteristics of children from dysfunctional families or from children who experienced trauma is that they are unsure of reality. Children, by definition, cannot validate their own reality. Their parents validate it for them. For example, the child may see the red lamp, and know it is red. But if the parent says it is orange, the child usually will agree (if the child is afraid)—even if somewhere in the back of the child's mind he/she was pretty sure it was red. But if someone walked by and asked, "What color is that lamp?" the child will probably answer, "orange".

When the child goes to the zoo for the first time and sees a zebra the child will probably call it a horse. The good parent says, "No honey, that is a zebra, a different kind of horse, one that has stripes." From then on the child can differentiate between a horse and a zebra. Reality has been validated in a positive way. When the child says, "I'm really mad at my brother!" and the parent says, "No, you should never be mad at your brother," then the child will learn to not validate his/her feelings and squelch them. If the parent says, "Yes, I can see you are mad at your brother, but you must not bite him," then the child's feelings are validated and the child will learn how and when to express them. This is how children learn to label and validate feelings and reality.

Abusive parents steer children to believe reality/feelings that allows the parent to manipulate and destructively control them. If the child's perceptions differ from the parents', the child is punished. The child soon learns that his/her reality/affect only get him/her into trouble. Solution? Buy the parents' reality/feelings—it's safer. *When faced with the fear/safety dilemma, one does what keeps one's world safe.* This same child grows into an adult who has trouble assessing and validating their own reality/affect. He/she has spent most of his/her life splitting his/her own feelings and reality and buying someone else's. This adult (who is still a dependent, scared child inside) learned long ago that believing what others want them to believe gets approval and safety. This adult is vulnerable to intimidation and control by others, and, somehow, controllers always find them.

With good friends and/or with therapy, this adult can learn to validate his/her own reality/feelings, and learn that validating them is important to being safe with one's self. As each little incident occurs where the choice is made to validate one's reality/feelings and run the risk of others not agreeing/disliking it empowers the person more and more into a strong, confident adult. The fear level drops little by little.

When children are raised in abusive, manipulative homes, they are in the ultimate fear/safety dilemma. They cannot leave. They fear their parent(s) but they love these same parents. Anyone who works with children's services knows the confusion and conflict of removing a child from an abusive home—the child doesn't want to leave! They are being hurt; but in spite of that, the child still loves and needs that parent.

So is it any wonder that in later life, as these children develop adult relationships, they already have an expectation that love and hurt coexist, that they have a "comfort level" or tolerance of the fear/safety dilemma already? They do not WANT to repeat the parental experience, but the dance they have learned with the parent(s) prepares them to repeat the system. Granted, there are people who get into fear/safety dilemmas who have not been in abuse/neglect homes, but for those who have it is a vulnerability that it may repeat.

Part of empowerment for "small" adults is to take their adult power to reconnect with their reality/feelings and to use them to make choices that effectively and appropriately meet their needs. Without validation of reality/feelings, there is little upon which to make choices. With good friends, with therapy, with opportunities to validate reality/feelings, these "scared children" can become empowered adults.

<u>Definition of child:</u> helpless, powerless, vulnerable, can't meet own needs, relies on others, no choices, safety rests in the hands of others, dependent.

<u>Definition of adult:</u> control over own life, makes choices to meet own needs, has power to protect and make one's own world safe, is only as vulnerable as one chooses, relies on self to know what to do (can accept information from others, but makes final decision internally), interdependent.

MAKING CHOICES

A choice that works well needs to be the combination of
REALITY + FEELINGS +OPTIONS = CHOICE

An adult needs to assess a given situation (reality), then look inside and assess the emotions about that situation (feelings), then assess the possibilities of what he/she can do in that situation (options), and from that a choice is made. The more a choice is congruent with reality, feelings and options the more peace, relief, contentment, strength and confidence one has. Obviously, for a person in the fear/safety dilemma, for a person who feels "small", validating reality, feelings and options is critical to making choices. One must be connected to one's reality and feelings in order to use them. Dominators do not want their subordinates to be connected and making choices—they want the subordinates to validate the dominator's reality/feelings/options. So if someone is caught in the fear/safety dilemma, validating reality/feelings/options in the presence of the dominator can be quite a task, but it can be done! But one needs support and skills to do this, and these are available. Empowerment is the key to resolving the fear/safety dilemma. Choice creates empowerment. Choice that meets one's needs accurately creates safety.

People are born with the capacity to assess reality—our five senses give us all the information needed to figure out what is going on and our brain puts it together rather well. Some families teach their children how to use this and the children become capable adults. Some families who want to control or dominate their children or who abuse them discourage or punish their children for doing this.

We are born with a full range of emotions and our families determine whether we stay connected with them and use them well or whether we split them for the sake of safety. What gets disconnected can be reconnected. The more connected we are with emotions and reality, and use them to exercise choice, the more empowered we are. When we are not connected to our reality and feelings, we are like a cork floating aimlessly in the water, directed by any wave that comes along, never knowing where we will end up, out of control. However, when we are connected to our reality and feelings, we are like well-anchored boats. The same treacherous waves will come along, but we will not move much. Let the storm come. A well-anchored boat will remain in the same place it was before the storm came. Storms are scary to corks. Well-anchored boats may not LIKE storms, but they know they will survive and will not be moved. Essentially this is the difference between fear (cork) and safety (anchored).

The goal of therapy is to assist people in building their own boats, finding their anchors. Support systems help people sail where they want.

What about the oppressors? What do they do when subordinates get stronger? The oppressor is used to getting his/her way and will not like it when this is foiled. Sometimes the oppressor will increase his/her methods to control to get his/her way. They still want to throw garbage into your yard. When "dances" (roles) change, toes always get stepped on—but it is survivable. Sometimes the oppressor will look for alternate ways to control (if force does not work, perhaps guilt will). It is definitely a battle, but for the subordinate, it is a battle for self, for adulthood, and it is worth it. Subordinates needs to be consistent in their empowerment until the oppressors "learn" that the old ways don't work anymore. Support systems are invaluable during this time—encouragement to just "hang in there" and not give in.

Sometimes if the oppressor is invested enough in the relationship—a parent, a marriage partner, an old friend, an employer—the oppressor may eventually change while the subordinate stands in his/her new empowerment. It is important to give the oppressor time to "hit up against" the empowerment and wait to see if, quite unconsciously, the oppressor realizes that if he/she does not change, the relationship will be lost, and they may not really want that to happen. They are faced with either altering their behavior or losing the relationship—change the dance or lose the partner. Unfortunately, the oppressors are so embedded in their controlling role that sometimes they are not willing or able to change. In that case, they will move on to find others they can control. Sometimes they can change enough that the relationship can be saved. Time will tell, provided the subordinate stays in the new empowered role and is willing to see what happens either way. Going back to the fear/unsafe role is not an option (actually it *is* an option but not one most people choose once they experience safety and empowerment).

CONCLUSION

Roberta's Role-Playing Situation Revisited

So where does this leave someone like Roberta, whom we met earlier in this chapter during the role-playing exercise? Her goal there was to lift herself up. Moving toward that goal means she is not going to adapt to her perceived smallness or to give in to her fear—as some people tried in the examples in Section Two. Instead, Roberta is going to assess her fear and deal with it by making herself stronger, using choice-making skills to reduce it. As she makes herself stronger, she will stand taller and eventually be empowered enough to confront the "fire breathing dragon." She will be able to consistently hold her own and not engage in self-destructive behaviors in efforts to handle the fear. The terror becomes deflated through her empowerment.

Together and Strong: What Most People Want

Most people, like Roberta in the role-playing situation, aren't looking for a way to end a relationship. They would like to stay in their relationships if at all possible. They realize these are their only parents, and they would like to keep interacting with them. Or they think fondly about their dating days and their marriage vows and don't really want a divorce. Or they like their job and would like to keep it and not let their boss's intimidation drive them away. They realize they have an investment in this relationship. But what originally appeared to be caring, respectful, or loving changed when fear crept in and the relationship dynamics changed.

Roberta had similar feelings, and we saw her learn to

- assess the level of fear

- flex her emotional muscles
- look to models
- validate her reality and feelings
- reach out for support
- become empowered until she became able to stand on her own.

These same liberating steps can become the experience of any person who lives in a relationship where the other person induces fear as a means of control. It *is* possible for the fear to be replaced by inner strength. As that strength is built up, the person who has been belittled and intimidated will no longer be crushed by the bullying tactics used to gain compliance through emotional terrorism. Empowerment and freedom from fear is what every healthy adult wants and needs. It is critical to having those satisfying, safe, happy relationships. It is the key to enjoying life and meeting its challenges with strength and gusto. It is possible to be together—and strong.

978-0-595-37427-4
0-595-37427-1

Printed in the United States
38842LVS00006B/616-759